To Darci —

Read with your mind —
Listen with your heart.

Thanks for all you do —
and who you are.

Love,
EV

Glimpse The Half

Poems

Ev Stransky

JoniArt Publishing

Book Design/Layout: Joni Oeltjenbruns

Cover photo Sculptor, Artist: Gregory Mendez

ISBN: 13:978-1718877672
ISBN-10:1718877676

DEDICATION

Within the pages of this book of poems, you will hear of three children who left this world before their parents. Adult children. But our children, just the same.

Though the poems here are not exclusively about losing children, I dedicate this book to all parents and children separated by untimely death — and the ones left behind who have to continue to walk the walk of Life. We know life is joy and sorrow; these pages embrace them both.

And for all who choose to take this little book of my poetry into their home or give it as a gift, my hope is that it will speak to your mind and your heart and your imagination. (And your funny bone, too.)

May you find peace, understanding and joy in the depth of art.

Ev

CONTENTS

ABOVE THE WIND

Above the wind

Are stars

Keeping silent watch

Being only

What they are

A distant presence

Visible

(or not)

GLIMPSE THE HALF

(Dawn's poem)   *Oct. 30, 2013, 2:00 a.m.*

If per chance you cast upon an angel's wing
adrift from high upon this earthly thing

then think you not a sore mistake
did make your wandering mind

then think you not it half broken from the whole
but pieced in part for purpose sole

when soul is drawn upon this sleeping place
to waken wonder not yet waked

and glimpse the half yet to be whole;

for even still upon this still wind fell
a message pure of kind

herald from a place afar your earthly reach
of purpose sent to rent the space

upon uncertain heart and mind meant to trace
its promised flight up and beyond.

A POEM WAITS

I

Sometimes, there's something just beneath the
surface
you can't hear it or label it or send your mind in
search of it,

but you sense it, just beneath the surface.

You look down, and over your shoulder,
knowing it may melt away any moment;

yet you feel an engine humming, just beneath the
surface
of the air you are breathing.

And maybe it's even gone for now,
hidden away in the universal storeroom—

maybe you didn't grab a pencil soon enough to
puncture
openings in the ethereal , just beneath the
surface.

You felt the vibrations against the thin skin of
your truth,
rumbling behind your awareness, just beneath
the surface.

II

A Muse? Is there another name I could give
this boundless visitor who claims a place in and
beyond

my finite little mind? One day again I shall find it
not quite sleeping and it shall claim its earthly life

riding, full front, on my fingers, opening portals in
my mind
as my heart stands witness with an urgency I
cannot explain;

only, when it breaks through the surface
it takes a piece of the embryo-me out into the air.

A ROSE ON THE MOUNTAIN

I will wander again through the hills of friendship

And taste the salty air of windswept memories,

Harkening deep the waves within my yesterday's soul;

And if per chance a mountain bloom appears

Upon my wavering path and spreads its fragrant petals

Wide enough to touch the steamy core, grown cold,

Then over again this day will serve a purpose pure

To feed the tiny stream a multi-foliate mountain rose

To glisten moist upon my arid earthen journey.

AMERICA AGAIN

Blessed are the tears
and the pain and the pride
of Man leaning down
to stand up and be better
than the moment of the bombs.

Blessed are the helpers
and the searchers
among the wounded
with cots and wheelchairs and water,

bandaging the blood
soothing the fear –
open hearts beating beyond
the 26-mile course,
beating faster than the
fastest runner.

Moments before: such joy
just to run, just to cheer, just to finish.

Moments turned: splitting
the air we breathe
making safety a foreign place,

pride dropped to the ground
like pieces of metal, and ball bearings
and nails – piercing more than legs
and bodies – piercing the soul of Boston

and once again, America stands up.
Blessed be America, again.

. . . and so came the previous poem: "America, again"

[April 15, 2013, the Boston Marathon was bombed by two brothers, originating from Russia.

3 people were killed, hundreds injured, many lost limbs. The bombs were ordinary pressure cookers filled with nails, and ball bearings. The oldest brother was killed in a gun battle with police. The 19-yr old was later captured hiding in a boat in a backyard; he was injured.

BABY RED FOX

I (Playtime)

Play – baby red fox
alive and well.
Five alive we've seen:
It seems a family
To romp and roll
Together – jumping, turning,
Making growth . . .
Playtime as they
Watch cars go by,
Or duck and hide.

II (Watching)

Ears pop up, round and wide,
Yet not afraid, inquisitive perhaps
Carefully searching the air.
We watched them, for weeks.
Romping, roaming, hiding, emerging
Close to their culvert home.
We often wondered where the mother was. Dead?
We never saw her surface with her pups.
Only five we counted in the sunshine.

III (We miss them)

There is a litter no more,
Not even one, visible.
Our eyes search for the one in our culvert
Who watched us come and go.
Our eyes search for the spots
Where they romped to our delight . . .
No more.

IV (We miss them)

Did they drown with the rains rushing the culvert?
Did they starve?
Did the coons get them? (the coons use the culvert,
too.)
Or – they say, "coyotes are killing off the fox."
Or did they simply grow up and leave?
I especially miss the one who ate curly fries.
Joe said they are meat eaters _
They wouldn't eat potatoes.
Nobody told the little guy as he
Snatched up the fry from the grass.

V (I miss my little one)

For whatever the reason
The little red fox went away.
I no longer look to the culvert everyday,
But when I do - I remember, and smile,
And envision something beautiful.

BLACK SMOKE

A distant message filled the morning air:
something terribly wrong.

Mind and heart escape the reality
of yesterday's peace;
this reality is black and billowing and devouring
the sky and space that belonged to a century
of Stransky families going about the business
of making a living, walking that very yard,
a yard now screaming a black symphony.

As I looked out my early morning window
from our now off-the-farm home,
the black smoke grabbed my sight
and smothered my heart
as the mind slowly comprehends
the terrifying reality: who or what
was feeding this ominous monster,
this rolling blackness taking charge
of what was once our home.

Prayer bled from my being

as the black smoke raged on.

The burning was in this farm-wife's soul

as the Stransky farm, in the distance,

where our son's family now lives,

was on fire. . .

Our prayers of thankfulness rose in the aftermath that

no one was injured and no cattle were lost. Our son's

family home, the barn, and all the other buildings were

saved due to a stellar job by three different fire

departments. Due to the wet, cool weather, the lack of

strong wind – (which was present before and after that

day), and due to the Grace of God.

BREATH OF MIKIE

The little boy
is only half-little anymore:
blond, blue-eyed magic
jumps into the back seat of our life
and we drive away
(if only for a moment)
to anywhere, to every where
the heart can travel.

Arithmetic (we used to call it) sprouts
from the quick mind of the eight year old:
"That one was too easy.
Give me a hard one."

A hard one is knowing the next time
he wraps himself into the seat belt of our world
he will be less the little guy,
slipping away from us
into a world of technology and robots
and finger-driven communications...

leaving us in a fog of
"How do you do that?
What do you call that?
How did you learn that?

Our world of baby calves
and hide and seek in the trees
and keeping balloons in the air
before they break while he laughs
and his sister laughs
and we laugh
and the world laughs...

is
becoming

a Grandma and Grandpa memory
of laughter and tears as we love—

as we love away the moments
of the little children growing:
our daughter's children

who is sending her breath

from Heaven
to touch the breath
becoming the big life
of the little boy Mikie.

She used to say
"Use your words, Mike"
when crying consumed
his little-boy moment...

and he learned to use his words
spawned by the love
of his mother...

His little-boy mind breathing on to manhood
may only remember her
(his mother of three years)

in the breath of his dreams:

be it, perhaps, her final gift
of many gifts given.

BROKEN

The mirror is broken upon the ground
and I cannot make a sound
as I walk the shards of glass
cutting the soul of my foot.

Yet I do cry out in silent scream,
not so silent it might seem
to those around the mess
made by shattered glass.

The drops of blood are poignant there
try as I might not to care,
clouding the image dull
the mirror shown before.

How long can a soul bleed its life
from a limb so scarred with strife?
I dare not think the price
this broken glass has cost.

But take this walk I must endure
though the mirror pains me sure –
there is reflection still
of what strength there once was here.

A PASSING CAR

There is a time
to drive the road
toward community:

a need to mingle
(or respond)
away from self,
toward motion . . .

There is a time
to remain
in the home of one.
shrink-wrapped
in the soul-self:
I call it, "just being."

I need the vehicle
which carries me . . .
when the shrink-wrap
begins to suffocate.

I need the privacy of me
when the community
rotates in circles,
endlessly seeking
the right color of home.

BROTHER AND SISTER

Swirling 'round in winter's Time
inhale the icy cold
with summer's warmth stored
inside the taut muscle's barricade
endure with inner fire
the frigid bites
so boldly born
always teaching . . .
imminent contracts of life's surplus
in family form;
from Nature's core siblings come
in contrast
clarifying potency in each other
by virtue of their own.

If you have welcomed warmth
absorbing her full
with trusting need
how can you deny
in its time
the cold breath of her brother's presence
kinship to your hearth?
Warmth would be a need
half known– a trite numbness
void of comfort had not her brother's
chilling strike
stabbed you wide awake.

COME AND VISIT

Come and visit my world.
You don't have to stay
if it doesn't suit you.

Just a visit, if you will.

Linger for a while and watch.
Listen to the sounds
before unheard to you.
Witness a way
different from your own.

And if
there is a moment —

A breath of redefined air;
a smile reborn;
light (or darkness) made visible;
knowledge of ways before unknown,
even if they aren't (or can't be)
your own,
Come and visit . . .

You may part an inch or two
from your yesterday-self,
and return home
suited in more flexible armor.

DARIAN

What's it like to be the tyke
bringing up the rear?
Tough and rough, scrape and scuff
with brothers three to fear;

taunting tears and nasty jeers
roll from your childhood face –
you'll show them sure, you'll find a cure
for being the baby last in place.

I

Trace the years my little man
and you may stand taller than the rest;
with tougher skin and races to win
to mark your space in the family nest.

II

Remember 'D' when you and me
would honor Dawn's place of rest;
with old rags in water warm
we'd gently clean the stone
'til it shown with the sun's love
and the love of our own.

III

In days to come
when Grandma and Grandpa succumb
to time that claims us all, we shall lie
beneath the sky near this precious stone;
I somehow know (with rags in tow)
my little tyke grown tall
will gently wash again the stone
in memory of Grandpa, me, and Dawnie.

DAWN

Eternal gift of morning
to spread across the day,
the beauty lies within—without,
and question though you may,
there is a form to guide your light
and bring the best to be . . .
Eternal gift of morning
enrich the lives you see.

from Mom

HS graduation gift

DIAGNOSIS/ DEPRESSION

O soul of mine kick the moon,
punch a hole in the sun
so it can cry too . . .

How dare the birds keep singing,
how ignorant they must be.
Bring tambourines into the silence,
arrogant silence! Thinks it owns
all the space, all the air,
every step that would be taken
toward tomorrow.

Who owns the corner
where the spider hangs?
insignificant, unimportant
little mite, not worth squashing
tonight – maybe tomorrow,
maybe never – but not tonight;
the moon has a headache,
the sun has sucked in its energy,
the silence sucks in any usable air,
as the steps meander –
or aren't taken at all
because lying down trumps standing up.
And the spider owns all.

DISTANCE

Distance is no longer a measure of away
when the train whistle resonates inside your mind –
like birds singing through the morning window
open to a begin-again-day of yesterday's world.

The separation of distance (here to there) closes rank
becoming one place in the mind: the away is here,
the distance evaporates and the unity of oneness
is the momentary reality, like making love,
like heaven and earth, like insanity.

Paul Tillich understood ,"The Eternal Now."
I understand only what a poet's mind is granted
in the fleeting moment when distance is no more
and the heart's capacity to feel takes over the space
from "here to there" : inside, eternal, aware.

I smell the lilacs, the fragrance is inside me.
I hear the birds, their song is inside me.
I see the movement of grandchildren, their joy inside me.

But sometimes – the heart breaks open
and pours out a silent sea
and creates a numbing distance
from a pain too great to see or hear or touch with the mind.

Sometimes – the distance away is the way
to survive. (God grant me"...Serenity...Courage...Wisdom...")

But in this moment – I must feel the train whistle,
the bird's song, the movement of little ones . . .IT ALL
fills the earth – and cries to the heavens.
        And there is no distance.

DO NOT GO DEEP

Do not go deep, too deep
    into the ocean,

Glide and splash upon the surface, safe
    from plummeting
    straight down to dark water.

Sunlight and ocean spray will keep you blinded
    as mysteries
    churn in half-sleep
    deeper that you dare to go.

Be life as you are, far from the ocean floor, buoyant
    from tethered kinship
    that would take you down
    to drown your fearful limbs
    in form of no return.

Do not go deep, not deep
    into the ocean;
    it asks too much
    it takes all
    in glistening darkness
    it absorbs all but remnants

and scatters you back to the surface – if at all –
    never the same.

In fact, the surface life
    may call you insane.

DULCIMER DANCE

One hundred strings
on soft bedded wood
2000 years in the making,
in ancient Persia
your dream dance began.

Carried across the ocean,
waves of soulful wind
bore you to transformation
on infant soil—
to dance your dulcimer dance.

Fluttering strings answer
the delicate hammering hand
gifted artisan offers;
his soulful movement gives you life
as Life you return to him.

Sing to my soul
ancient merriment;
transcend the time
of your and my beginning;
dance, dulcimer, dance.

DWELLING

The sea's home is itself,
its place on the planet.
We like to think the tide
that comes to shore is "coming home."
Is it our need to call the coming –
"home," while the sea retreats
to its own reality?

The sea's Being is its home.
Can we learn more from
this great mass of moisture,
beyond its moon-directed ebb and flow,
beyond its rage and calm,
beyond wonder and awe,
beyond its beauty and secrets –

Can we learn, like the sea,
that the heart has its place fixed
within, pulsing life: the ebb and flow
of nourishment and waste,
of excitement and sorrow,
of accomplishment and defeat,
of entering and exiting.

Like the sea ,
the heart's home is itself –
while you are but its cradle
moving around in the world.

EARTHBOUND

What this a sorry angel's face
held vast upon a vaster place
with earthly ties of mud and mire
a tedious road; too soon to tire.

Upon the curves that gently veer
not so gently breaking near
this way to tread without a wing
this strange and curious earthly thing.

If feather soft could but take hold
sweet memory's songs within the fold
would wisp sway the wing at morn
with cloudless wind of time reborn
in movement free with cleansing throng
angelic voice could claim the dawn
if dawn were held to hearken here . . .

Not yet to be, not yet so near.

ELDERS OF THE TRIBE

Put on a new face for the visitors.
With so many new faces, so often fabricated,
which face is real –
the us they yearn for us to be?
Why is what we were so wrong?

At the core of "our town" – who are we?
At the tail-end of "our time" – who are we?
Externals ever changing, ever emerging
in the passion of progress;
internals stampeded over, leaving dust as the legacy.
What are we chasing, changing to be?

An unrecognizable store front
for the elders of the tribe to pass by
with tears in their eyes, wiped away
with calloused hands. Where to shop and stop
and remember who we are?

So short a time we stand with knowing identity
before progress raises its ravenous head
and feeds upon old morsels, not enough.

EPILOGUE

Is reality a rock, always to be
beaten away by cascading waters
from new-born clouds
demanding their space in time -

If so, there Is no rock-reality,
only shifting sands,
camouflaged for the moment
as hardened strength.

If so, strength is but an ever
changing wave upon a

yielding stone-shore
to become someday sand,
someday desert –
as we yield our bones to sand
and all dry up and blow away:

All as it should be –
All is reality.

New rocks shall form.
New rain shall fall.

A poem written for Sister Franchon; written to be sung to the tune of, "What Child is This"

FRANCHON

What smile is this
that came to rest
on suffering souls
before her . . .

She walks in light
to calm the night
and lend her love
before us.

She, she is sent from high
to move in places far and
nigh;

Now, here we share a
while
God's Breath behind her
smile.

GRANDSON'S BOOTS

(for Roamer)

I smile at size three, and maybe a seven by now,
And a five, perhaps; and one with no shoes at all.

The big toe points west inside the rubber boot pointing east;
Chubby legs don't care. No time for particulars.
Cement steps and surprises on the ground need to be navigated
Before the big outdoors is postponed by a mother's call.
Mothers have schedules;
hands on the clock point to appointments
Not to be ignored.

Grandmas play in grass and
push on the swing ten-times-sky-high.
Sometimes, between giggles,
the boot pointing east flies off.
The big outdoors doesn't notice.
Only Grandma watches it fly through the air;
She watches, too,
where it lands how many feet from the swing.

Grandmas are like that:
having navigated the big outdoors long enough
To know that boots will be piled in a corner,
too many to count;
And smiles come one at a time,
sky-high with giggles, too many to count.

But Grandmas can count slow,
and store numbers in an unscheduled place
Only they can go.

HERE NOW AT 59:

Bird voices ratchet the air;

Surround-sound in serenity:

My backyard.

I'm older now.

I use moments to place my ears

Toward the sky . . .

Moments which yesterday

Were shrouded in movement:

Cattle chores, committee reports,

Lawn mower belts, car engines

Starting and stopping and starting again.

Line-dried diapers competing

With dust bunnies –

For my movements to task.

Stopping now—means stopping

Not a quick head turn as in

My yesterdays.

This movement now of my deck swing

Beholds harmony with the air.

Where birds sound-paint the dome

Beneath which I sit – quietly –

Absorbing the voices of . . . peace.

God has blessed my decades:

Babies, banners, box office,

bathtubs, box stalls and birds,

The birds quicken the air

Of this moment, now,

And I listen, and I am here.

HIGHWAY 35W BRIDGE COLLAPSE
August 1, 2007

It's never over, a disaster.
The smoke clears, the fires die down.
The sun comes up. But it's not over.
The grim searching continues . . .

Curious people stand looking, looking,
as close as they can, as close as they are allowed.
Comprehension: a foggy anomaly
somehow different from the movies:
this rubble is real; their skin senses something
Hollywood fails to capture:
Terror is a moment of truth
played out in as many ways as there are eyes
beholding what life (and death) can be.

The *soldiers* have been at work from the moment
The CALL came, drawing them into a place
called Reality. Their bodies become machines
doing what they've been trained to do;
not yet letting emotion freeze their movement,
not yet. It's not over. It's down, but it's not over.

Gurneys haul the injured
supported by any hands there to help.
TV reporters, road blocks, rescue boats,
fireman and police and EMT's
are not just men and women – they transform
into symbols of hope: they are here, they know
what to do, because it's not over.

Tomorrow, heavy equipment will heave forward.
Doctors will give updates; police will re-route;
the experts will open their files. . .
recovery workers will need food, and water,
on a hot Minnesota day.

The media will begin their feeding frenzy
The distant-lucky will watch from their living rooms,
and read from their chairs,
and drive to work somehow more alert
knowing the bridge is gone, and knowing it's not over.

Someday the bridge will be rebuilt.
Someday thousands of cars filled with people
in their ordinary pursuits will travel again
with little thought of disaster.
Someday, this tragic event will be absorbed with
sunshine
and new water flowing beneath our senses.
Logic assures us that someday this all will be over;
Reality will regain its composure.

But today, a school bus rests on the edge of
what was left of the bridge:
A symbol of mercy (by whatever God you name)
for all of the children survived.
And they will know, at the core of their remaining
days,
their own personal picture of disaster: a moment of
truth
that's never over – never truly over...

HIS NAME WAS JOHN

His name was John. Did you know him?

He was a husband, a father, a brother, a Marine.

But, for this poem, he was a son.

Did you see him:

walking his dog, mowing his lawn,

playing with his children, dancing with his wife?

He had a smile that could melt wax.

Being a man meant, being a man.

Did I mention, he was a friend?

Did you notice his stride, his eyes,

his voice when he laughed?

He knew how to step up to the plate – of life.

Did you value him in uniform?

Did you know his enemy did not carry a gun?

      His enemy was cancer.

      He was 43 years old.

His mother talks of him loving

the snow, the cold, when he was little:

he'd play outside for hours with a red smiling face.

His mother stood on the hallowed ground

of Fort Snelling Cemetery, in the blistering cold.

Her heart knew it would be so.

Her tears moistened the ground where soldiers lie,

where her son would lie – after the taps,

after the flag folded in the arms of his wife;

mother looked on in the cold moist air

of saying goodbye. Did you feel it?

Her name was Mary -- His name was John.

HOW OFTEN A MASTER

Shakespeare had an ear
for music of the pen,
he played with reckless candor
inside the hearts of men.

Tho many may distain him,
their hearts in trappings be,
the rhythm of his soul
is heir to set us free.

HUDSON RIVER MIRACLE

We need miracles.
We need to know, to be sure;
sight, sound, touch: the receivers, the in-your-face
tactiles of God's reality – that being saved is possible—
all 150 of US, standing on the wings
of an airplane sinking, slowly into the Hudson River
on a frigid day in January.

There were pictures – taken from a distance—
of the living bodies standing
like wet, cold, toy soldiers, shoulder to shoulder,
on the arms of their could-have-been tomb.
Instead, the arm of God buoyed their lives
to live another day.
We have pictures of the "miracle" on the Hudson
River.

The news media is good at getting "pictures."
More often pictures of the pain:
Kosovo, Iraq, Sudan, Tsunami, 9-11 . . .
But today, the pictures are different –
tug boats, ferries, helicopters, divers,
the story-book images of the rescue,
the miraculous rescue,
the boats converging closer and delicately closer
to the floating tomb-become-sanctuary.
It looked to me much like a circle
of humanity circling 'round Humanity.

Did you see it? Did you see it on TV, or on your computer,
or on your blackberry? Did you *See* God? If not,
did you perhaps feel a tingle on your skin,
a heaviness in your throat; your jaw ajar
in disbelief at what had just happened?

Did you see the pictures? Hear the words? Read the
stories?
They said, "It was a miracle:" the skill of the pilot,
the lack of strong winds, the help of strangers,
the plane holding together in one piece, etc. etc. etc.

Were you there?
They said the people prayed . . .
Why is prayer what we do before we hit the water?

We do so need miracles we can see:
the big-before-your-eyes ones; the ones that have
brothers and mothers and children
who surround us every day in subtle shadows
and work clothes and soft baby sighs;
the multitude of miracles we seem to step over
like stones on a beach
 (or ignore like engines propelling a plane.)
 Why is it these are not enough –
Why is it we need the big-before-our-eyes ones
every so often to jolt us awake?

Jesus knew – Miracles Teach.
We need to see, hear, touch ...... be saved.
We need miracles to remember,
as we remember God.

I'M AFRAID OF MY WATER SOFTENER

I'm afraid of my water softener:

you have to set dials on the two
thing-a-ma-rounds, two hours apart
(if you forget and set them on the same time –
. . . I have to stop and think what will happen.)

there is a long cylindrical thing on the left –
the one that looks like a torpedo, only smaller
(or bigger, depending on what war you're fighting.)
there is a fat tub in the middle that holds
salt pellets (or you can use granular – but they say
that dissolves faster – I don't really know
because I've never had the nerve
to use granular. I'm frugal. I don't like to
waste things, even salt.

I was told that the two cylinders (torpedo tanks)
MUST be set to regenerate at least two hours apart
or there will be a chemical-hell-to-pay.
There is purple stuff, in the small tub on the floor,

that has a tube connected to the first torpedo

(something like an umbilical cord – if you have

an imagination.) I think the purple stuff

was named by a puffed-up chemist.

"Potassium Permanganate."

(does "toxic" have a significant meaning here?)

I was told if the fluids in the two tanks

got mixed together……." it would not be good." (like

Napalm and fresh air – mixed together. Not good.)

I don't really know…….I'm not sure I've

figured it all out properly.

What I do know is that the older I get

the more afraid I am

of the water softener: it somehow owns a piece of my

safety……that used to be free (like fresh water.)

Navigating freedom was so easy when I was young.

I never used to be afraid of water softeners.

I'VE NEVER BEEN TO PARIS

I've never been to Paris. Never had a need to go, I guess.
Had the opportunity fallen before me, I think even then no
strong calling would have drawn me away from where I was.

Home is a powerful place to be. Roots that feed the body
and soul nourish stability. Something the wanderlust folks
have not tapped into – anymore than I find connective-life-
tissue in far-off adventures.

Oh, traveling to places and sights new to the senses can be
enjoyable, enlightening, fascinating – for the moment, yet
something akin to tulips blooming in the Spring: the splash
of color is short-lived, then other flowers take over their wilting
presence. You know anything else like that?

A breathtaking building can only hold your breath at bay
for so long. Then you breathe again, your own normal air.

Hoards of distant, unique people, or a handful of captivating
charmers can grab the attention for a while –

But all people sleep (though in differing beds);
eat (though their own foods); cry (with their own private tears);
and laugh with a universal face.

Some folks give, some take. Some care, some have lost caring –
or never learned it to begin. Some have accumulated great
knowledge,
some—who perhaps have never left their birth place –
have great wisdom.

Home is not a place in particular. It's a state of stability, a feeling of comfort in belonging. It's an aura of peace in where you've chosen to be. I've never been to Paris, and probably never will be.

IN MY BACKYARD

My Grandson said,
"Grandma, what's that sound?'

I wondered if the birds were aware
of the little creature below their perch;
they were busy breathing out
their existence in sounds
the angels wrote and sent earth-bound
for little Joseph's ears . . .

He knows the sound of train whistles,
and water, and grass: their sound
Is distant, and wet, and green.
But today, the lesson was birds:
making their presence
a surprising sound he heard
in my yard – in his life.

The continuum of birds
and water and grass
and grandmas and grandsons—
will be the angel's mission
long after . . .
when Joseph and I, together
become a new song sung
for a little boy's ears
in his grandma's backyard
where birds will breathe again.

KATRINA

What an oxymoron it is to give a hurricane
the name of a beautiful woman. Ripped
lives form lines of frustration; tender eyes
are open sores, deepened by fear when the
winds and water come.

Her arms have no tender touch. Her mouth
spews no sweetness when the wind-driven
rain pelts every visible object, like bullets
demanding their target – and all is target.
Escape is the only lover suitable to the moment.

The meaning of "home" temporarily
transforms – leaves the senses – softness and
safety are no longer an option in the face of
her fury; the familiar face of daily existence
has been blown to bits.

The elderly say, "I want to go back to my
home." – to yesterday, to youth, to
innocence, trust in tomorrow and the
"things" which defined my life.

The little ones clutch their blankets or a
stuffed toy taken up in the last moment of
departure. Their sense of home is yet
forming; their loves are yet to come.

Thousands huddled in the Superdome as Katrina wrapped them in her presence. Rain falling through the tattered roof of their temporary lives forces them to fear, to pray, to hope – and to know that tomorrow will never be the same.

Katrina was strong. Those who survived the pain of her destruction will absorb her strength and know her for the oxymoron she was.

All hurricanes should be called Jack-The-Ripper, with numbers to follow.

MY FIRST TRUE POEM

I see a dim light gleaming
Of a palace in the sky,
And someday I will go there
To that palace up so high.

I'll climb the highest mountain
And rest upon her peak,
For there will lie my kingdom
And that is what I seek.

I'll dance among the meadows
And sing among the birds.
I'll play a harp in heaven
For there I'll need no words.

I'll play among the ocean waves
And sit upon the shore,
For God has given me a life
Of which I could ask no more.

My first true poem, written when I was in 5th grade.
The teacher gave me an "F." She said I couldn't have
written it – I must have copied it from someplace. I did
write it, walking down a back field road, heading for
home at dusk. It came straight from a bursting heart; it
came out in metered foot. I have no idea how. I had no
idea what poetry rhythm was back then. It just felt
right. It was right.

JELLY JARS

Jelly jars a jam'n
wait'n with their lids,
sit'n on the counter top
rows of juicy kids.

Rim-brim'n jelly jars
suck'n in their seal,
wait'n for their tops to pop,
what a fruitful deal!

MY TEAR

My tear

cascading down

the mountainous cheek

of my being

falls to a pool

headed for heaven.

NIGHT RAIN

It's the sound
sizzling bacon
if I listen without looking

The rain-song
claims my senses
as it claims the sidewalk darkness.

Thunder orchestrates
its chosen moments
overwhelming the crisp rain's voice

Adding percussion
in rumbling overture
magnificent movement across the sky:

Movement of its muscles
(and mine)
frying the sky

As the rain keeps beating
its sizzling symphony
straight-down-all-around-sound

To ignite
the dry burner
of my quiet, too content mind.

ON THE PORCH

Open sky, moon above

Soft-milk clouds, distant love

Breeze of night, gentle touch

Star and moth, feel so much.

NOTICING ME

My tongue is pushing up against my teeth

As I awake in the morning.

I don't remember that being a reality

In my twenties. Maybe—I was

Too strong, too fast, to notice.

Flabby skin on my lower arm

Wasn't there, either, in my youth.

I'm noticing some changes these days,

Like the ever-enlarging knuckle

On my right forefinger. I remember noticing

Hands that spoke loudly of "old age"

On old ladies—so, so different from mine, back then.

I'm noticing those brown spots

On my face, never there before - - - not on my

Clear and soft skin—skin that now plays host

To whiskers austerely growing wherever they crop up.

The "crop" on my face now grows on the field

That once hosted adolescent embarrassment.

But I can walk.

And still dance (for a while).

I can shower and relish

The soap, the water, the warmth

As I turn and turn and close my eyes and mouth

To let the water have its way with me.

Diabetes has come; so has the lap top.

Food comes in many forms.

I am fed.

OLD TREES

They answer the wind in movement

Because they are.

A butterfly, high in the branches,

Touches . . . ever so gently,

Softly brushing their hair—

Because they are.

The sun paints shadows;

Their faces respond with majesty and magic –

Because they are.

Old trees stand sentinel

Along my backyard, shoulder to shoulder—

Because they are.

They stand with nobility of the years:

Silent knowledge innate,

Preaching only with their presence;

Peace, perhaps—

Because they are.

I am their witness – because they are –

And the clouds overhead say, "yes."

PICTURES

They took pictures . . .
that traveled the world.
    And it was too much
to take in
with the pictures being so clear:

the arms and legs and blood
vivid with new technology
so we all could see
pictures of the pain . . .

    And it was so much
that our sensory cells
became clogged with feet dangling
and smashed heads and children
alone on dusty, leftover streets –

and vacant eyes looking
beyond unrecognizable rubble
into the lens of a camera
for a picture
they did not understand,

    for it was simply too much
to take in
with nothing clear – except the pictures
flying around the world
at cyber-speed.

And we said, "Did you see the pictures?"
    And it was too much . . .

And the snow outside my window
is so clear.

How deep can the camera's eye reach?
How clear the picture?
How fast can you dig
with your hand?

PIN IT ON THE DONKEY

A childhood game to make you laugh
where foolish was fun –
unless you didn't like to lose,
unless being the closest to
the rear end of a donkey was
somehow a crucial victory in your mind.

The victory *was* in your mind;
of being the best, the center of it all
by blindly finding the significant
tail's end – when the significance
of it all was quickly forgotten by
the other children as they rushed
away to new distractions,
leaving you standing there
alone with the donkey's
tail between its legs;
the big moment of pride only
an echo of children's laughter,
yet an echo everlasting
in some remote chamber of your soul.

POETRY: SUNG AND UNSUNG

Poetry is the soul singing . . .
crying
questioning
announcing itself
    in splendor
        in agony.

It is not
work. But it works the poet,
and if he directs its outpouring purpose
for eyes and ears other than his own,
it indeed becomes estranged labor,
    not song;

for what song there may be
is only half sung
and the soul retreats
    in silence,

awaiting
its freedom-flight
through the essence
pure of the singer
who writes (not alone)
the song of himself,
    joined by Eternity's choir.

SALUTE TO FREEDOM

There is something sacred

in the morning moment

when the flag is raised,

and the wind takes charge

of the message.

If you can hear with your eyes,

"homeland" is a transcending wave

from places afar,

(whether you were there or not.)

You are here.

And that makes all the difference

in the world.

SERVICE OF OLD CLOCKS

The old clocks,
the ones that went
'round and 'round
instead of blink, blink –

there was reassurance
in that circular motion,
and rhythm
in the "tick-tick-tick-tick" –
like the heartbeat of a healthy
mother going about the business of giving;

or the heavy steps
of a soldier's boot
on a very hot day,
hard and heavy and hoping
to stay in stride with a rhythm
that might someday
save his life, or – offer it up.

Old clocks are a reminder,
a sound for the soul,
listening to time
yet never owning it;

just a steady report,
like wind whipping clothes
on a summer's day clothesline – or
the rhythm of artillery
in a dark, foreign night.

SHE ASKED HIS NAME

My brother is dying.
I told my bible study group this morning.
I told them, almost in passing,
"He is my mentally handicapped brother."
They all said with words or faces
that they were sorry.
They all said, mostly via our leader,
that they would include him in their prayers.
They are good people, they mean to be Christian.

But one woman: the mother of a handicapped child,
ASKED MY BROTHER'S NAME.
She asked his name –
and I knew there would be a prayer for Laurell
carried to God by angels, for their sister
wanted to know his name.
The power of this question
changed the air around her ... and me.

And the rainbow I saw on the way home
was vividly real,
as was this woman who knew it was important
to know his name.

SIMON, WHERE HAVE YOU WALKED TODAY?

Simon,

where have you walked today?

Along the streets of vacant vision:

tattered faces peering blank

from cardboard boxes,

hands outstretched

piercing naught but dead air? – certainly not you,

Simon, for you have seen it all too often.

Where have you walked today, Simon?

Amidst majestic pines;

homing birds of freedom with wind-filled wings,

trilling songs to sweet air?

Just where have you, Simon, walked today?

Along the ocean line,

wetting your eyes far out to sea

while white sand stayed clinging

to your smooth, wet ankles?

Simon, can you tell me where you walked today?

In valleys of sunshine

freshened by the green

and colored life

of flowers in the breeze?

What form of nature have you seen, Simon?

Have the trees or birds or valleys or ocean waves

sung their song to you, Simon,

as you walked today?

Was it pleasant, Simon, that you could walk to –

And away?

SNAKES IN A PIT

Only gruesome

to the outsider

looking in;

when it's home

with well-worn paths

to and from,

slime and curling bodies

are the norm,

the coziest place to be.

SOMEONE TOUCHED ME

Someone touched me along this path of Life.
I turned, and there was a smile.
I fell, and there was a hand for me to grip.
I won a prize, and there was joy springing from the
shadows.
I sorrowed, and there was a heart to catch my tears.

Someone touched me along my way,
and I learned to be more than I was.
Endurance is not taught by unending pleasure.
The prickly fingers of pain guided the process of my
strength.
I was touched and taught –

And age was not a factor.
Maybe it was the cradle that I rocked,
or the graying hair that I combed,
or the encouraging words I kept in my back pocket,
or the letter I tucked away and saved.
Maybe it was a warm bowl of soup brought forth
to soothe a shaking body.
It could have been the simple sound of a door opening
And footsteps again making full the room of my
existence.

In all and any case, someone touched me,
And Love found a place to lay its precious body.
Lives intersected upon this Earthly home
and brought rays of joy interspersed with rays of pain
to light my world with the kaleidoscope-touch
that only I remember—

for I have the privilege and the pain
of holding in my heart the precious gift
of that someone -- who touched me.

written for Hospice, May, 2004

SUMMON THE SURPLUS

Even in winter's cold
snow abounds with reason
demanding endurance
summoning strength
wetting the appetite
for warm summer sun.

Let the contrasts live
creating in their vast extremes
the valued middle ground
stored within.

Of rich mellow warmth
there would be no sense
if bitter winds did not bite
their identity
upon our consciousness.

Absorb the presence

of now –

be it hurting cold

or warmth caressed.

For each season is in surplus

in its now.

Store it well

so tomorrow's turn

will find your senses

fortified, ready

to love—or endure.

SURVIVAL

He walks, with shoulders loose,

upon the hidden echoes

of twigs and crisp decay

covered by night the light

of his eyes knows well;

stealth movement born

from ancient wisdom

deep in muscles, taut,

yet smooth rippling waves

kissing the ocean of his being,

his kind, the uncertain future.

And seated behind the fire

we only see his shadow,

or is it his ghost –

the fear, the promise

of predator, of prey.

SWING HARD THE GATE

Swing hard the gate of foreign thought

Lock the latch and lead me naught;

For daylight leads the dreams astray

But dark of night will flood the way

With torrents daft of rational thought

When only peace of sleep I sought;

Swing hard the gate in Satan's way

And steal me not as helpless prey;

I end the days with hope of slumber

When whirling mind flails rest asunder;

SWING HARD THE GATE, I pray thee come,

Hold out the demons to save this one.

TAKE OFF FROM AMSTERDAM

They walked through the lives
turned to rubble –
the missile found the mark,
too high in the sky to be
accidental.

And the world turns
same as yesterday.
Only not the same
for the people
in the rubble –
for the people
left behind to cry
to the gods of carnage
"Why?"

What if my senses fail me
as I watch through the rubble
too often to calculate the cost?
What if the "Why?" burns dim
with cold ashes,
and I forget to cry?

*(Malaysia airliner with 298 passengers was shot down
in Ukraine)*

THE OLD COUPLE IN THE TWO STORY HOUSE

One wonders

in winter

how to keep

the cold out

from the two

story house.

At the center

of it all

is an old

furnace.

THE BLUE JAY AND THE SQUIRREL

A comical sight –
the surprise of it halted me;
no more than a second or two,
but none the less eternal,
as if Napoleon drew his sword
in my backyard.

I had turned just in time to see
a momentary "stand-off"
between a blue jay and a squirrel,
each defending his identity, it seemed.

A flash upon the grass, a tumble and roll;
A statement of "I AM."
Be it fur or feather, each was
born to be who he was in that moment;
    makes no difference blue or gray
    "I am – make way!"
This flash of the absurd,
the bird and the squirrel in battle,
externally so different –
but in this moment, so the same.

My attention was welded by
some invisible bond I could not break.
The flurry froze in my sight

80

and strange as it may seem
I sense it may be stored somewhere
in my mind;
an electrical imprint of some eternal truth,
some lesson to be learned with eyes wide open.

The blue jay eventually flew back to his tree,
and the squirrel again tended the ground of his acorns.
And all was right with the world –
at least in my back yard.

They say the ocean is present in a drop of water,
and all information in a particle of DNA.

Could it be –
that the battleground of mankind
has its replication in the backyard of our lives?

I ask for the wisdom of my backyard inhabitants
to stand the ground of identity
yet move to resolution without losing the "I am."

God made the bird to fly.
God made the squirrel to dig and climb.
He put both in my backyard.
Or perhaps, I am in their backyard –
the backyard is a very big place.

THE DISCIPLINE OF WATER

Running faucet:

falling warm

then warmer

to the hot position

makes me

understand the

big difference

of cold.

YOU ARE WELCOME HERE

Come and sit.
Be not alone.
You are welcome here.

Bring all of you.
Yourself the gift.
Words, eyes, being.

Share your day.
Remember pieces.
Speak words unspoken.

Silence may come.
It has a place.
Do not fear.

The voice inside
may find its way
when the Way is needed.

Eyes can laugh
when crying has
no more a claim.

Come and sit.
Be not alone.
Do not fear.

You are welcome here.

*In July of 2005, terrorists bombed London —
the worst since WWII. My thoughts turned
toward our own 9-11. I sent this poem to the
Prime Minister of Great Britain, Tony Blair. I
received a letter back from his office.*

Where You Are

The sun was shining in Minnesota,
and probably California,
when the subways blew
and the bus exploded:
Churchill's beloved London, revisited.

The new generation cried out;
young voices who had learned
to trust the sun, choked on shadows
in the bowels of their city —
onlookers saw the bus
regurgitate its cargo into
what was once their morning air;

while the old voices
of New York's children
said, "I hear you . . ."
and the smoke traveled across the ocean
and entered their windows
and their eyes — and they too
began to look up at the darkened sky.

10 DOWNING STREET
LONDON SW1A 2AA

From the Direct Communications Unit

28 July 2005

Ms Evelyn Stransky

USA

Dear Ms Stransky

The Prime Minister has asked me to thank you for your recent letter and poem.

Mr Blair appreciates your kind thought in writing.

Yours sincerely

R. Smith

R SMITH

YES I WILL

Someone died today,
yes they did.
I hear the rattle of the coffin cart
as I'm watering my flowers.

My next door neighbor
is a mortician –
the rattle comes at all hours.
I sometimes stop what I'm doing
and look through the trees
as the cart is hooked to the vehicle
to journey toward its destination.

In a few weeks
Daria will have her baby –
and I will be a grandma
for the fourth time,
Yes I will.

WOUNDED

There are noises
like a wounded animal;
almost whispers with no rhythm.

hearing the sounds....
coming from where?
behind the wall – ?
with tiny bursts of air

like a bicycle tire
going flat, only sporadic
like a secret leaking out
from somewhere deep
in a well – yet somewhere
just beneath the surface
the sound comes forth, softly;

and as I lie quiet, I know it's coming
from me.

WORKSHOP

What invention am I?

Soaring bird-spirit

With crawling-thing legs?

Experiment

In the combination of

Bacteria bathing in earthly soot;

Molecules moistened with heavenly tears:

Ever building and destroying

The holy mud of me.

Body and Spirit

Created

From yesterday's tomorrows;

Crafted

Especially, delicately, purposely

for

Today's

Marketplace

While soaring, soaring

toward

Eternity.

WITH EYES WIDE OPEN

Is it a huge dream, O Lord, from which
we will awake
and in its wake
over-see the final plan
the initial, eternal, final man?
If it be so,
let me sleep, O Soul of mine,
with eyes wide open
in trust of the dream.

WHEN YOU BECOME UNDONE

When you become undone

Quit!

Go and Sit
by a window.
Look
at the crook
in a leafy tree.
See
the sparrow
homing the sky

free-falling but not to die . . .

sit—look—see
Quiet
is free
like the sun

when you become undone.

WHEN APPLES FALL

Adam screams
from beneath the Tree
"How long, Lord?
must we feel naked?"
The Tree of Life – of good and evil –
makes no answer.

    Today, 2006, in Pennsylvania,
    five little Amish girls
    are gunned down in their simple
    country school: execution style,
    bound, bullets to their heads.
    The chosen ones.

    Together, they died;
    together we die
    so alone, Lord,
    beneath this damned tree.

    My heart beats
    in their blood.

    Your blood, Lord,
    is the only way out
    of that school house; Your tree
    the only tree that can bear
    the weight of this day,
    and the days
    yet to come . . .

WHEN THE FLOOD CAME

What mind has the river
taking the place of our lives?
no mind, only movement
determined
by forces called Nature (which way the god?)

dykes break
with our hearts, and lives;

sandbags brace
heavy objects of hope against the unknown
power
of the river;

actually no river, anymore,
only vast water
seeking its own boundaries no one can see;

houses, cars, puppies
flower beds, baby beds,
someone's diary . . .

no matter to mindless muddy movement
overtaking sewers, sedimentary waste
then – and now;

cattle can only swim for so long,
then become mindless objects
floating, bloating
given to the river
run amuck amidst yesterday's lives;

backyards ..... barnyards .....
ball fields ..... corn fields .....
main street stores ..... playground swings .....

all surrender in the space
as we take our place

rescued or not
to wait and wonder
and re-build life
in the dry land of our minds;

distant observers send money,
as ducks swim
wherever the water resides ,

wherever
the every-so-often
mind of the water-god
floods our lives
with a highly visible
"I AM."

WEEPING

Weeping is a solo hymn –
Tears can't be shared
        like jelly beans in a jar;
external as they are
tears belong to the soul:
they burn from the inside – out ,
while sparked from the outside – in,
to be ignited on tender kindling
        where burning is a solitary thing.

Be not ashamed
when the soul sings its solo hymn –
for tears can purify a dusty heart,
and comb through tangled emotions;
        silver strands emerge
            straight falling
                salty pure
                    gravitating down

only to evaporate
into heaven's realm
to become a reservoir
for all men's tears to come.

After all, "Jesus wept"
a solo hymn
a reservoir
a communion
for all Man's tears to come.

WATER SYMPHONY

I, an open vessel,
as water flows around me,
sun streaks finger their shining tune
upon the wet
and rolling surface surrounding
the me in half light,
witnessing the majestic
playful tune: brilliant rays
moistening the air
inches from my mind.

A water symphony
carrying its own tune
while silently carrying me;
ripple-vibrations circle 'round and away
from the nucleus – mine –

soundless, reaching out
to the infinite and ringed
moist lips of the wetted sun
making its music upon the water:
The Singer flowing 'round me,
the Sound almost within reach –

as I sail . . .

USED TO BE

Used to be

DARKNESS in the room
engulfed me;
a surround-sound of black,
nothing
but acute awareness
of myself, alone.

Used to be

DARKNESS was a deep breath
owning the void of vision;
a shroud to my sight-sense,
no point of reference
for my eyes to embrace.

DARKNESS that used to be
is dotted now with technology,
birthing little points of light
punctuating the solitude
(that noble emptiness)
of my 2:00 a.m. house:

TV dot over there, smoke detector up there,
telephone charger right there. . .

My eyes are open now to a new space.
My inner eye, once embracing darkness,
has been extinguished by intruders:
little points of light, necessary here
as living change. . .

The moon now has competition.

TO KENDRA, FROM GRANDMA (WHEN I'M GONE)

Kendra, show me what you look like.
Stand in the sun on a warm and vibrant day
And I will see you clearly in the warm glow of your life.

Kendra, show me what you feel like.
Run through the grass, your feet pounding the ground
Strong and sure (like your mother's feet would run),
And I will feel your strength vibrating the earth.
And when you roll in the grass with your puppy, I will feel
The soft touch of your skin and I will know again
The softness of love, young and pure.

Kendra, show me when you hurt.
Lift your face just high enough and I will come
As a gentle breeze to dry your tears, for I too have cried.
And if the hurt is great, and darkness fills your space,
I will rest at the foot of your bed and we will await the
dawn together.

Kendra, show me what you dream of.
Big waves of far-off oceans, or that boy who makes your
heart pound
When he looks your way; I will talk with God and we will
make a plan.

Kendra, show me your whole and beautiful self
As you walk through this precious journey of your life,
And I will hold close your flaws
and imperfections right next to
The sound of your beating wings as you fly strong
With the purpose God gave you the day you were born –
The day your mom was born – the day I was born.

Kendra, show me, and I will be there
With eyes of love and pride from sunrise to sunrise,
Keeping watch over God's perfect plan:
You. Kendra. Show me.
And you will feel my answer in the touch of the wind;
And see my spirit in the glow of the candle; and hear my love
In the cooing of the baby you hold in your arms.
Kendra, show me what you look like and we will never walk alone.

THERE MUST BE SOME POETRY

There must be some poetry
yet to be written,

There must be some ear
yet to be smitten,

So write on, my Poet,
my captor, my king;

You could do some greater – or
some lesser thing.

THE WINDMILL

If there is spirit

in that which we call Life,

then know it first

in God's breath upon the earth,

the unseen that moves

through the fields of wheat,

through the hair of loved ones'

through the turn of windmills.

All things, in their turn,

reflect the breath of God;

all things, still or torrent,

embrace the spirit,

our first breath and our last.

THEY ALL ASKED IF I HAD A GOOD TIME

I walked on sacred ground.
A sign warned of snakes.
It was the Wild West, you know.
Untamed, except for the information building,
complete with toilets and sinks and
automatic soap dispensers.

Apart from 21st century amenities
I stood on sacred ground: feeling
that knowledge as I gazed across
the grassy hills of heated July –

the same hills where Indians united
their tribes, coming from all directions
to surround the enemy, the intruder,
the white-skinned, forked-tongue soldier
whose bones would be found on this hill,
and moved to Washington, D.C. for
what honor escapes me
as I look out over the sacred ground
where hundreds of white markers
stand in the sun and the rain and the cold.

And the grass of the sacred hills surround

the information markers telling of the battle:

Custer's Last Stand.

It struck me square on – like the bite of a rattle snake –

that some brave souls came forward

just twenty-some years ago to erect

a few scattered "red" stone markers which spoke

for the hills: "Here lie Indian remains."

And I knew only the hills held the sacred truth

of this weary and wonderful land.

THE VISITATION

In the middle of the room sat strength,

bejeweled in a simple string of pearls

circling a slender neck held straight and proud.

Her hair, her wool suit: all was in order.

She was the mother who told her daughter,

"Of course I'm coming . . ."

She was 99 years old.

(Marge smiled as she told me about the exchange.)

Marge the wife, standing;

Leo the husband, lost his face-off with cancer;

and the amazing Mother: a trio of life lived fully.

One, moved on.

One, trying on new skin as a widow.

One, the ageless matriarch sat in an aura of

quiet strength – of having survived long past "being old,"

into a place of grace, hovered over by the angels.

At 99 she emitted a message, ageless, of hard earned grit,

of down-home country common sense. Of dignity.

She sparkled with the energy of kinship when

I told her we too were farmers.

I saw her, in truth, for only a few minutes.

I saw the truth in her for probably my whole lifetime.

She was a rare gem bejeweled in pearls.

She unearthed my soul in a way I may someday

be privileged to understand – if I live to be 99.

THE TRUCKER

TRUCKER, TRUCKER
WHERE DO YOU ROAM,
CLAD IN JEANS
SO FAR FROM HOME?

TRUCKER, TRUCKER
HOW MUCH WILL YOU PAY
HASHBROWNS AND EGGS
AT THE ROADSIDE CAFÉ?

TRUCKER, TRUCKER
HOW SWEET IS THE GAME
PLAYED WITH THE WAITRESS
WHEN YOU KNOW HER BY NAME?

TRUCKER, TRUCKER
WHAT DO YOU SEE
WHEN STARING AT STRANGERS
OR THE CURVE OF HER KNEE?

TRUCKER, TRUCKER
IS IT LONELY AT NIGHT
WITH EYES FOCUSED ONLY
ON THE RIG'S STEADY LIGHT?

TRUCKER, TRUCKER
HOW MANY SMILES
DID YOU LOG ON THIS RUN
OF CROSS-COUNTRY MILES?

TRUCKER, TRUCKER
WHEN DO YOU SLEEP
WITH MILES YET AHEAD
AND CONTRACTS TO KEEP?

TRUCKER, TRUCKER
DOES YOUR MIND WANDER FAR
WHEN YOU SEE A LARGE FAMILY
PACKED SNUG IN A CAR?

TRUCKER, TRUCKER
DO YOU WISH IT WERE THROUGH
THIS LIFE ON THE ROAD,
WAS IT CHOSEN FOR YOU?

TRUCKER, TRUCKER
IS IT TRUTHFUL TO SAY
YOU DO THIS FOR REASONS
APART FROM THE PAY?

THE TRIAL

O.J. Simpson was acquitted; the bloody murders left unsolved.

6 months after the trial –

"I do believe he was guilty,"
said Kato's little-boy face:
the face that was there.

Fear
has its own private tentacles
gripping deep and firm.
Silently, it kills
all forms of witness.

. . . he was there, so verbal, so silent.

II

There was a cross – somewhere –
placed on a hill, a playground
of the times,
bathed in shouts and fear.

. . . little-boy faces were there, afraid.

Little boys have to grow up – somehow –
their playground bathed in trust and truth,
or knives and nails and lies will keep killing
little boys to come . . .

Fear:
the tentacle binding hard our hearts,
closing our eyes, stilling our humanity,
to be not there.

Truth was lying in blood on a sidewalk –
Truth was hanging on a cross before our eyes –
It was there.
We were there.

III

At the time of the trial
how easy it is to utter,
with our little-boy faces,
"I do not know him."
Oh, but we do my people,
    we do.

    Why is it so long
    after the trial
        that
        we do?

ZACH

The guys at the farm used to call you, "Zach Attack."
I call you a marvelous mystery,
a secret under its own shell,
moving in the world at your own pace,
sure and steady.

Do you know the "Midas Touch" story?
...where everything he touched turned to gold:
a wish granted by the power that was. Forget
the greed part, focus on the gold; the rare gift
meant to serve you well, and (if my prayers come true)
will serve the needy world well, sure and steady.

My mind's ear hears you:
"My name is Zach and I don't look back."
My mind's eye sees you:
Athlete in a jersey, white show clothes,
master of the machines.

As with your brothers, my heart- light will forever
hover over you, the shell blessed to move in the world,
sure and steady, with God in your ear and Grandma
waiting to hear the mysteries you will share.

To Allan and Randee Radel in memory of their beautiful son,

Scot Baek Radel

The Season of Searching

The season turns,
and grips me unaware.
All is changed.
I walk in a foggy dream
whose curtains I cannot tear open.

The sun refuses its warmth.
Sleep shows no friendship,
it sneers at my weariness.
I want only to wake, united.
And walk home, together.

The days have stollen the hours.
The hours have become the enemy.
I walk the vast terrain of hope.
Filled rooms, empty places.
Each day I cry.
Each day I rise, heavier than the last.

So many faces come; so many
arms and eyes and voices:
they want to help ...
So many prayers; I cannot pray alone.

II

The season turns.
The cameras have gone.
I return to the place called home.

I am confused
and tired and grateful
for all the people —
their candles, their flowers,
their prayers ...
but I am confused.
I want to understand.
I want to know!
It hurts too deeply not to know.

I now walk numb, in a skin
foreign to me.
Food has lost its joy
and become only a necessity.
I cannot fill this empty pit.
I cannot silence
the silent scream inside me.

Hunger is an urge not to rest
until I know.
The noise of my questions

riddle the night.
So many questions ...

III

I don't have words.
I don't want words.
How is it the words
in my mind will not cease?

This is so beyond words —
sometimes silence
is the engine of my heart:
power-driven by pain.
Being alone is the cage

I choose to enter.

IV

We, as a family,
did all we could.
We kept reaching, and trying,
banging against the empty space
of the unknown.

But we defied the unknown.
We worked so hard . . .
We did all we could do
in that dark moment.

V

Friends, and strangers,
carried our hearts on their shoulders.
They were as angel-dust
powdering our souls.
We could lean hard and not fall.

Fate, the fanged controller,
did not defeat us;
it stole from us, but it did not defeat us.
Scot felt our hearts — searching,
doing all we could.
In whatever remote way — he knew.
We are family — he knew.

VI

The season turns.
Someday I will know.

Someday I will understand.
But not today.
Today I will learn, slowly,
how to walk in a new skin
because of my love for my beautiful son.
I taste the richness of that love
in a way as never before.

I've met the angel,
with swords hidden in her pinions,
but none the less an angel
who leads me to re-live, re-remember,
and to learn again to stand
on solid ground and breathe new air.

And my tears will become
holy sepulchers.

VII

There will be seasons to come . . .
I know not when or how;
but there will be seasons to come —
when the purpose of my son's beauty
will light the sky with warmth,
and I will stand strong and proud.

THE SCRIPT

We try
and fall so short
of making it perfect, of having it be as we dreamed
it would be.

All of us – even those pictured perfect
behind the neighbor's camera lens –
when the curtains are closed,
can ache of failure in a play rewritten without our
permission.

We can't direct this mess!

The actors
aren't moving where they're supposed to . . .
they don't get the lines right. (and there are so
many lines missing)

Wasn't it supposed to be lighter in here?

"Divorce? Not in my family?
Depressed? How could she be?
She had so much, we bought it."
All of us – we bought it for so long.

He wasn't supposed
To die
To leave
To be deformed
To get fired
To run away
To have cancer

THIS IS NOT THE RIGHT SCRIPT!

Eventually,
we learn to move from the director's chair,
and take our place within the audience
to let the play evolve . . .

as Reality writes itself.

Be assured,
the Director's chair
is not empty,

THE RIVER

On a clear and happy day the river caresses its
boundaries: the welcome feel of flowing in a pathway
known and trusted to be true.

And then life turns on its side, taunting the river with a
dark cloud that invades the sun's domain,
demanding its time, shrouding its way over the happy
day ....

and a cold and cutting rain ignores the boundaries
birthed by the river – and the rain comes down hard
and hurting, and overflows the bank. The safe and
happy path the river claimed as it own is no more.

And all is changed.

The water rages with foreign objects afloat, and what
once rode the river in safety and joy is washed
away, for the certainty of a pathway is gone – nothing
is as it was.

And first we cry. And those tears belong to the river,
and the river will carry them as holy water to
mix and mingle with a thousand other tears of those
also with a right and reason to cry.

Can I be angry with clouds? Can I say to the river,
"Stay your course! Do not cover my homeland with
debris that I may not have the strength to clear from
my soil, my home, my heart."

And as I wait, afraid, and angry with this water
drowning the dreams – the river is patient, knowing it
will again find the boundaries which made it a river –
which made it life –

And though the shoreline may be altered, the soil
shifted and redefined – the river will reclaim its
boundaries, and flow in a pathway trusted again.

For life travels with banks and boundaries, and when
the storms take away logic, and visible pathways,
the river itself never gives up its birthright –

And just beneath the surface, just beneath the chaos
and the hurt, the core of Mother River is steady in her
path. And in time, she will draw back onto the place of
her beginning –

And her banks will again be visible, and the sun will
again shine, and my tears, and what suffering came to
pass, will serve the river as it journeys on, taking a
piece of me with it.

And its never-ending movement – the movement of
Life – will carry me forward, and I will trust again the
boundaries; the river's flow; and the sun's/Son's
immense power to heal.

(For a Hospice Memorial Service, May 2011)

THE FALL OF LOYALTY

I pass it every time
on my way to town
on county road 45;
the rolled up clump
is there, is noticed –
if there aren't other
distractions like cell phones
or face to face conversations
with my husband.

It must have been
going about the business
of being a raccoon
when it was hit.
Up the road, maybe 45 feet,
another clump on the same
side of the pavement –
no doubt searching
for its mate
which it used to meet
face to face.

THE GATHERING

He died.

They came.

For their own reasons.

The combines moved

Up and down the neighbor's field.

Huge, churning statements

Of pride and giving

And being who they

Could best be.

The sight was worthy of

Bringing in the plow

And halting my own tillage

To behold

In dead silence

The Season of Harvest.

ABOUT THE AUTHOR

Does Poetry Matter?

Does poetry matter? For me, it does. Many times poetry has probably replaced "Prozac" in my attempts to face sorrow and help it move on. In moments of overwhelming joy, poetry has given a voice to thanksgiving. And those times when my world was too complicated to comprehend, poetry has served me well as a ship navigating a rowdy sea.

When I was in 5th grade, I completed an assignment (while I was walking down a field road at dusk) to write a poem. I got an "F". The teacher was quite upset. She accused me of "copying it." She said that I could not have written that poem. It was in metered foot. I didn't know what metered foot was, not did I copy anyone's poem. I've kept that poem with me (in my purse) for over 40 years. It was the beginning of my use of poetry to help me walk my life in harmony with myself, and attempt to make sense of the world around me.

So many major events, on the world stage or on my stage, I have chronicled with poems: happenings dated, delved into, delighted with, devastated by . . . I can tell you the year Susan Smith drowned her two little boys, and I can tell you something about this mother's questioning of what sanity is and what the lack of it means . . . it's in the poem.

Days and nights I've been moved to write: the death of the Kennedys, Martin L. King Jr., Princess Diana, my mother and my handicapped brother; the disaster of the space shuttle, Columbine, Oklahoma City, Katrina, Kosovo, 9-11. Because of having put into words my attempt at digesting the 9-11 experience, I re-visited that poem when London was bombed in 2005. I felt a connection to the people of that city (and country) and was compelled to write. I sent it to Tony Blair, Great Britain's Prime Minister at the time. I received a sincere letter of appreciation from 10 Downing Street.

When things happen which touch my being – poems appear: a poem about O.J. Simpson. For years I had admired his stellar ability in football, and his camera-ready charm. Then reality was turned on its head and I had to process this transformation (in my mind) from macho to monster. When Captain "Sully" landed his plane safely on the Potomac River, a poem wrote its way through my tears of joy and appreciation for heroes, and miracles, and the gift of lives spared when so many others were taken that year. I ached for the sadness of Michael Jackson's childhood which never seemed (in my perception) to end. I wrote a poem about a man/child. It connected me to something larger than his fame and unique talent.

I wrote a poem after sitting in the ER with my first grandson under a "Code Blue" – a poem was the only way my heart could say thank you to the medical staff, and to God. I often pray with poetry. I looked into the face of my last granddaughter and knew my mortality was in her eyes. I wrote a poem I may not be here to see her read and understand.

Does poetry matter? I have to believe that if it can help me navigate life, process life, illuminate life, cry over life, worship life- then I have to believe that it does the same for others who observe life closely and see poetry (and art) as Man's way of becoming one with a universe larger than himself.

As someone once said, "I write because I have to." I so understand that statement. Just as something moves a painter's hand, Mozart's notes were in his head, placed there by a power beyond himself.

Does it matter, poetry? Did Shakespeare matter? Did Monet or Renoir? Did Beverly Sills or Karen Carpenter or Louie Armstrong or Elton John – did they, do they matter?

If, as I have seen and felt, poetry (and art) has the power to bring emotional well-being, or a new-light understanding, or the right to question, if only for a moment – or for centuries – then it matters.

I am a poet. I matter. People remind me of poems I sent them years ago, now folded and tattered, stuffed away in a drawer, (the "stuffed away' part is what matters) – like worn teddy bears – or the first poem we dared to write or dared to love.

Thanks

- to Joni Oeltjenbruns, author, artist, optimist: skilled navigator who kept urging me on – telling me, "it's your book." It wouldn't have happened without you, girl.

- to Gregory Mendez, extraordinary sculptor who created ' one-winged angel' on the cover of this book, which inadvertently was connected to the "Glimpse The Half" poem, which (I believe) had a connection to our daughter, Dawn. And thanks to the Owatonna Health Care Campus, where the angel now resides as a piece of healing art.

- to Katherine Baumgartner, who was 'Kathy' the first half of our lives. She changed who I was because of who she is. She taught me to value the light of a candle.

- to Joe. When I stumble, he's there to break the fall. When I'm frustrated, he's there to 'take it on the chin.' When I fly, he is the horizon, his smile is my destination. He is – my HOME.

Made in the USA
Lexington, KY
14 July 2018